MCA MUSIC PUBLISHING

ANDREW LLOYD WEBBER   TIM RICE

EVITA is an opera based on the life story of Eva Peron, the second wife of the Argentine president Juan Peron. Eva Duarte was born in 1919, illegitimate, poor, without privilege. She became the most powerful woman her country had ever seen, the First Lady of Argentina at the age of 27. She died in 1952 of cancer, aged 33.

ACT ONE

It is the 26 July 1952. A young Argentine student, Che, is among the audience in a Buenos Aires cinema when the film is stopped by an announcement that Eva Peron, "the spiritual leader of the nation, has entered immortality".

Eva's funeral is majestic, a combination of the magnificent excesses of the Vatican and of Hollywood (REQUIEM FOR EVITA). Huge crowds, much pageantry, wailing and lamentation. Che is the only non-participant (OH WHAT A CIRCUS).

Che in EVITA is at times a narrator, at times an observer, at times simply a device that enables the authors to place Eva in a situation where she is confronted with direct personal criticism. There is no evidence whatsoever that Che Guevara ever met Eva Peron or became in any way involved with her, but the character Che in EVITA is based upon this legendary revolutionary. He was, however, an Argentine born in 1928 and would therefore have been 17 when the Perons came to power and 24 when Eva died. He became strongly opposed to the Peronist regime during Eva's lifetime and it is not unreasonable to suppose that his later activity in Cuba and elsewhere was in part a reaction against the government he had known in his youth.

Flashback to 1934. A night club in Junin, Eva's hometown (ON THIS NIGHT OF A THOUSAND STARS). Eva Duarte is just 15. She asks the singer appearing in the club, Agustin Magaldi, with whom she has had a brief affair, to take her to the big city—Buenos Aires. He is reluctant (EVA BEWARE OF THE CITY) but she gets her way (BUENOS AIRES).

Once in Buenos Aires, Eva quickly disposes of Magaldi and works her way through a string of men, each of whom helps her one rung more up the ladder of fame and fortune (GOODNIGHT AND THANK YOU). She becomes a successful model, broadcaster and film actress.

1943. Colonel Juan Peron is one of several military leaders close to the presidency of Argentina which in recent years has proved a far from secure job for its tenant. (THE ART OF THE POSSIBLE).

At a charity concert (featuring Eva's old friend Magaldi) held to raise money for the victims of an Argentine earthquake, Eva and Peron meet. They both realize that each has something the other wants (I'D BE SURPRISINGLY GOOD FOR YOU). From now on Eva hitches her ambitions to political stars. She evicts Peron's mistress from his flat (ANOTHER SUITCASE IN ANOTHER HALL) and moves into Peron's life to such an extent that she excites the extreme wrath of two factions who were to remain her enemies until her death—the Army and the Aristocracy (PERON'S LATEST FLAME).

As the political situation becomes even more uncertain it is Eva rather than Peron who is more determined that he should try for the highest prize in Argentina—the presidency, supported by the workers whose backing she and Peron have long cultivated. (A NEW ARGENTINA).

ACT TWO

Eva's ambition is fulfilled and from the balcony of the Casa Rosada on the day of Peron's inauguration as president (4 June 1946), the vast crowd gives Evita, now Peron's wife, an even greater reception than that accorded to Peron—thanks to her emotional and brilliant speech and to her striking appearance (DON'T CRY FOR ME ARGENTINA). Che notes and experiences some of the violence that was never far away from Peron.

Che asks Eva about herself and her success but does not meet with a great response (HIGH FLYING ADORED). Eva's main concern is her forthcoming tour of Europe (RAINBOW HIGH) which begins in a blaze of glory in Spain but meets with later setbacks in Italy and France. She never gets to England at all (RAINBOW TOUR).

On her return home, Eva resolves to concentrate solely on Argentine affairs, undeterred by continual criticism from the society of Buenos Aires (THE ACTRESS HASN'T LEARNED THE LINES YOU'D LIKE TO HEAR). Che points out that the regime has to date done little or nothing to improve the lot of those Eva claims to represent—the working classes.

Eva launches the Eva Peron Foundation (AND THE MONEY KEPT ROLLING IN AND OUT), a huge concern of shambolic accountancy and of little practical benefit to the nation's economy although it helps to elevate her to near goddess status in the eyes of some of those who benefited from the Fund—including children (SANTA EVITA). Che's disenchantment with Eva is now total. He sneers at those who adore her and for the last time tries to question her about her motivation and the darker side of the Peron administration (WALTZ FOR EVA AND CHE). Eva's response is that of the pragmatist. "There is evil ever around, fundamental." She has realized that she is ill.

Anti-Eva feeling among the military reaches new heights, and Che lists several of the major failures and abuses of the Peron administration. Peron attempts to justify her domination of Argentine life. He draws attention to her illness (SHE IS A DIAMOND).

Peron and Eva discuss the worsening situation—he is losing his grip on the government, she is losing her strength. Eva refuses to give in to her illness and resolves to become vice-president (DICE ARE ROLLING).

But the opposition to her from the army is too great; more importantly her body lets her down. She knows that she is dying and makes a broadcast to the nation, rejecting the post of vice-president, a position she knows she could never have won. (EVA'S FINAL BROADCAST).

In her last hours, images, people and events of her life flow through Eva's mind, while the nation's grief knows no bounds—to the mass of people she has become a saint, nothing less. As her life draws to a close she wonders whether she would have been happier as an obscure ordinary person. Maybe then her life would have been longer....(LAMENT).

But even in death she is denied obscurity. The moment she dies the embalmers move in to preserve her fragile body to be "displayed forever", although this never happened. The story of the escapades of the corpse of Eva Peron during the quarter-century after her death is almost as bizarre as the story of her life.

This Night Of A Thousand Stars

MUSIC BY ANDREW LLOYD WEBBER

Lyrics by
TIM RICE

MCA MUSIC

Eva, Beware Of The City

Music by ANDREW LLOYD WEBBER

Lyrics by TIM RICE

1. E - va, be - ware of the ci - ty___ It's hun - gry and cold,___
2. Five years from now I shall come back___ And fin - al - ly say,___
3. *See additional lyrics*

can't be con - trolled, it is mad:___ Those who are fools are
you have your way, come to town:___ But you'll look at me with a

swal - lowed up whole, and those who are not, be - come what they should not be - come
for - eign - er's eyes The mag - i - cal ci - ty a young - er girl's ci - ty, a

changed___ in short they go bad. **Bad** is good for me I'm bored so clean and so ig - nored___
fan - ta - sy long since put down. **All** you've done to me___ was that a young girl's fan - ta -

9

3. Eva beware your ambition: It's hungry and cold —
Can't be controlled, will run wild;
This in a man is a danger enough,
But you are a woman, not even a woman,
Not very much more than a child —
And whatever you say, I'll not steal you away!

Buenos Aires

Music by ANDREW LLOYD WEBBER

Lyrics by TIM RICE

Lyrics for Dal Segno (repeat)

3. You're a tramp, you're a treat, you will shine to the death, you are shoddy;
   But you're flesh, you are meat, you shall have every breath in my body:
   Put me down for a lifetime of success
   Give me credit – I'll find ways of paying:

   Rio de la Plata etc., as Coda

I'd Be Surprisingly Good For You

Music by ANDREW LLOYD WEBBER

Lyrics by TIM RICE

1. It seems cra-zy but you must be-lieve there's no-thing cal-cu-la-ted, no-thing planned. Please for-give me if I seem na-ive. I would ne-ver want to force your hand: But please un-der-stand, I'd be good for you.

in like this Twen-ty sec-onds af-ter say-ing hel-lo. Tell-ing strang-ers I'm too good to miss. If I'm wrong I hope you'll tell me so: But you real-ly should know, I'd be good for you.

2. I don't al-ways rush

MCA MUSIC

Another Suitcase In Another Hall

Music by ANDREW LLOYD WEBBER

Lyrics by TIM RICE

MCA MUSIC

Additional Lyrics

2. Time and time again I've said that I don't care;
   That I'm immune to gloom, that I'm hard through and through:
   But every time it matters all my words desert me;
   So anyone can hurt me and they do.

   So what happens now? . . . . etc., as above.

3. Call in three months' time and I'll be fine I know;
   Well maybe not that fine, but I'll survive anyhow:
   I won't recall the names and places of this sad occasion;
   But that's no consolation, here and now.

   So what happens now? . . . . etc., as above.

Don't Cry For Me Argentina

Music by ANDREW LLOYD WEBBER

Lyrics by TIM RICE

out of the win-dow, stay-ing out of the sun.   So I chose free - dom

Run-ning a-round try-ing ev-ry-thing new, but no-thing im-pressed me at all,   I

never ex-pect-ed it to.   *Slow Tango feel* *Refrain* Don't cry for me Ar-gen-ti-na_____ the

truth is I nev - er left you: All through my wild days,   my mad ex-ist-ence,   I kept my

love you and hope you love me. Don't cry for me Ar-gen-ti-na Mm m m

Don't cry for me Ar-gen-ti-na_____ the truth is I nev-er

left you: All through my wild days, my mad ex-ist-ence, I kept my prom-ise, Don't keep your

dis · tance___ Have I said too much? Theres no-thing more I can think of to say to you

But all you have to do is

look at me to know that ev-'ry word is true

High Flying, Adored

Lyrics by TIM RICE

MCA MUSIC

Instrumental (Solo)

EVA

High fly-ing, a-dored, I've been called names but they're the stran-gest

My sto-ry's quite u-su-al —— lo-cal girl—— makes good, weds fa-mous man—

Rainbow High

Music by ANDREW LLOYD WEBBER

Lyrics by TIM RICE

EVA: I don't real-ly think I need the rea-sons why I won't sus-ceed,___ I have done! Let's get this show on the road, let's make it ob-vi-ous Pe-ron is off and roll-ing

BEAUTICIANS: Eyes! Hair! Mouth! Fi-gure! Dress! Voice! Style! Move-ment! Hands! Ma-gic! Rings! Gla-mour! Face! Dia-monds! Ex-

MCA MUSIC

EVITA is based on the life of Eva Peron, the second wife of Argentine dictator Juan Peron. She was a girl from the most ordin[ary] of backgrounds who became the most powerful woman her count[ry] (and indeed Latin America) had ever seen, a woman never content [to] be a mere ornament at the side of her husband, the President. He[r] death of cancer at the age of 33 in 1952 ensured that the loved, hated, inspiring, corrupting complexity that was Eva Peron became a legend.

Patti LuPone

Mark Syers

Jane Ohringer

Mandy Patinkin

Bob Gunton

And The Money Kept Rolling In
(And Out)

by ANDREW LLOYD WEBBER

Lyrics by TIM RICE

Waltz For Eva And Che

ANDREW LLOYD WEBBER

Lyrics by TIM RICE

CHE

Tell me be - fore I waltz out of your life, be - fore turn - ing my

back on the past;_____ For - give my im - per - tin - ent be -

hav - iour, but how long do you think this pan - to - mime can last?

She Is A Diamond

Music by ANDREW LLOYD WEBBER

Lyrics by TIM RICE

PERON. 1. But on the o - ther hand— she's all they have_____
2. & 3. See additional lyrics

She's a dia - mond in their dull___ grey lives, and that's the hard -

- est kind of stone— it us - ual - ly sur - vives

And when you think a - bout it, can you re - call___ The

MCA MUSIC

last time they loved_____ an - y one at all?_____

star   She's the one___ who's kept us   where we are___

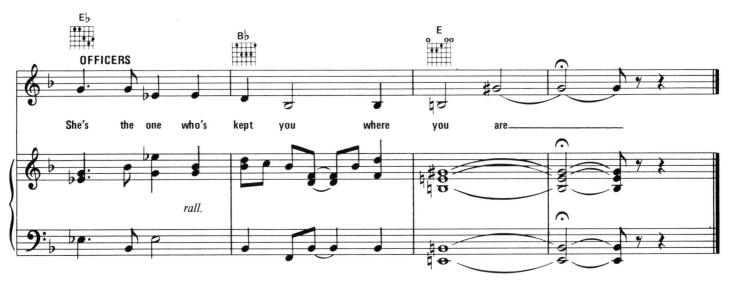

OFFICERS

She's   the one who's   kept   you   where   you   are_____

rall.

Additional lyrics

2. She's not a bauble you can brush aside
   She's been out doing what we just talked about, example:
   Gave us back our businesses, got the English out
   And if you think about it — well why not do
   One or two of the things we promised to?

3. But on the other hand, she's slowing down
   She's lost a little of that magic drive — but I would
   Not advise those critics present to derive
   Any satisfaction from her fading star
   She's the one who's kept us where we are

   (Officers)
   She's the one who's kept you where you are.

EVITA

ACT ONE

1. A CINEMA IN BUENOS AIRES, 26 JULY 1952

An audience is watching a less than distinguished movie (in both the original London and New York productions of EVITA a clip from one of Eva Peron's own movies was used). The soundtrack dialogue is in Spanish, the music melodramatic. Suddenly the film grinds to a halt. The people in the cinema begin to protest but are silenced by an announcement:

THE VOICE OF THE
SECRETARY OF THE PRESS

It is the sad duty of the Secretary of the Press to inform the people of Argentina that Eva Peron, spiritual leader of the nation, entered immortality at 20.25 hrs. today.

2. REQUIEM FOR EVITA / OH WHAT A CIRCUS

EVA's funeral. CHE is the only non-participant. He moves through the mourners, apparently unseen.

CROWD

Requiem aeternum dona Evita
Requiem Evita
Evita   Evita

CHE

Oh what a circus! Oh what a show!
Argentina has gone to town
Over the death of an actress called Eva Peron
We've all gone crazy
Mourning all day and mourning all night
Falling over ourselves to get all of the misery right

Oh what an exit! That's how to go!
When they're ringing your curtain down
Demand to be buried like Eva Peron

It's quite a sunset
And good for the country in a roundabout way
We've made the front page of all the world's papers today

But who is this Santa Evita?
Why all this howling hysterical sorrow?
What kind of goddess has lived among us?
How will we ever get by without her?

She had her moments - she had some style
The best show in town was the crowd
Outside the Casa Rosada crying 'Eva Peron'
But that's all gone now
As soon as the smoke from the funeral clears
We're all going to see how she did nothing for years!

CROWD

Salve regina mater misericordiae
Vita dulcedo et spes nostra
Salve salve regina
Ad te clamamus exules filii Eva
Ad te suspiramus gementes et flentes
O clemens o pia

CHE

You let down your people Evita
You were supposed to have been immortal
That's all they wanted
Not much to ask for
But in the end you could not deliver

Sing you fools! But you got it wrong
Enjoy your prayers because you haven't got long
Your queen is dead, your king is through
She's not coming back to you

Show business kept us all alive
Since 17 October 1945
But the star has gone, the glamour's worn thin
That's a pretty bad state for a state to be in

Instead of government we had a stage
Instead of ideas a prima donna's rage
Instead of help we were given a crowd
She didn't say much but she said it loud

And who am I who dares to keep
His head held high while millions weep?
Why the exception to the rule?
Opportunist? Traitor? Fool?

Or just a man who grew and saw
From seventeen to twenty-four
His country bled, crucified?
She's not the only one who's died!

Sing you fools? But you got it wrong
Enjoy your prayers because you haven't got long
Your queen is dead, your king is through
She's not coming back to you

CROWD

Salve regina mater misericordiae
Vita dulcedo et spes nostra
Salve salve regina Peron
Ad te clamamus exules filii Eva
Ad te suspiramus gementes et flentes
O clemens o pia

A non-descript GIRL moves through the pageantry of the funeral. She sings as the voice of the dead Evita:

GIRL

Don't cry for me Argentina
For I am ordinary, unimportant
And undeserving of such attention
Unless we all are - I think we all are

Ride on my train o my people
And when it's your turn to die you'll remember
They fired those cannons, sang lamentations
Not just for Eva, for Argentina

Not just for Eva, for everybody
So share my glory, so share my coffin
So share my glory, so share my coffin

CHE

It's our funeral too

3. ON THIS NIGHT OF A THOUSAND STARS / EVA AND MAGALDI / EVA BEWARE OF THE CITY

Flashback to 1934 and to a nightclub in Junin, EVA'S home town. EVA DUARTE is fifteen. The cabaret is nearly over. MAGALDI is singing with great gusto.

CHE

Now Eva Peron had every disadvantage you need if you're going to succeed. No money, no class, no father, no bright lights - there was nowhere she'd been at the age of fifteen, as this tango singer found out. A tango singer! Agustin Magaldi - who has the distinction of being the first man to be of use to Eva Duarte

MAGALDI
(The final song of his act)

On this night of a thousand stars
Let me take you to heaven's door
Where the music of love's guitars
Plays for evermore!

In the glow of those twinkling lights
We shall love through eternity
On this night in a million nights
Fly away with me!

I never dreamed that a kiss could be as sweet as this
    - now I know that it can
I used to wander alone without a love of my own
    I was a desperate man
But all my grief disappeared and all the sorrow I feared
    Wasn't there anymore
On that magical day when you first came my way
    Mi amor!

On this night
On this night
On this night of a thousand stars
Let me take you to heaven's door
Where the music of love's guitars
Plays for evermore!

MAGALDI joins EVA and her family - mother, 3 sisters, brother - at their table. CHE is loitering nearby at the bar.

EVA

To think that a man, as famous as you are, could love a poor little nothing like me!

MAGALDI

The audience here are sitting on their hands

CHE

Listen chum, face the fact they don't like your act

MAGALDI

But this is Junin! If this were Buenos Aires - I'd have that town at my feet! I never ever meet members of the public - they'd tear me apart!

CHE

'I understand their feelings

EVA

I want to be a part of B.A. - Buenos Aires - Big Apple!

EVA'S FAMILY

She wants to be a part of B.A. - Buenos Aires - Big Apple!

CHE

Just listen to that! They're onto you Magaldi! I'd get out while you can

EVA

It's happened at last - I'm starting to get started - I'm moving out with my man

MAGALDI

Now Eva don't get carried away -

EVA

Monotony past - suburbia departed - who could ever get kicks in the back of the sticks?

MAGALDI

Don't hear words that I didn't say

EVA'S FAMILY

What's that? You'd desert the girl you love?

MAGALDI

The girl I love? What are you talking about?

EVA'S FAMILY

She really brightened up your out of town engagement, she gave you all she had - she wasn't in your contract -you must be quite relieved that no-one's told the papers -so far...

EVA

I want to be a part of B.A. - Buenos Aires - Big Apple! Would I have done what I did if I hadn't thought, if I hadn't known, we would stay together?

CHE

Seems to me there's no point in resisting, she's made up her mind, you've no choice. Why don't you be the man who discovered her? You'll never be remembered for your voice

MAGALDI

The city can be paradise for those who have the cash, the class and the connections - what you need to make a splash. The likes of you get swept up in the morning with the trash - if you were rich or middle class -

EVA

Screw the middle classes! I will never accept them! And they will never deny me anything again! My father's other family were middle class and we were kept out of sight, hidden from view, at his funeral! If these are the people of Buenos Aires I welcome the chance to shine in their city!

CHE

Do all your one night stands give you this trouble?

MAGALDI

Eva, beware of the city
It's hungry and cold, can't be controlled, it is mad
Those who are fools are swallowed up whole
And those who are not become
What they should not become
Changed - in short they go bad

EVA

Bad is good for me - I'm bored, so clean and so ignored
I've only been predictable - respectable!
Birds fly out of here so why oh why oh why the hell
    can't I
I only want variety - notoriety!
I want to be a part of B.A. - Buenos Aires - Big Apple!

FAMILY

She wants to be a part of B.A. - Buenos Aires - Big Apple!

MAGALDI

Five years from now I shall come back
And finally say, you have your way - come to town
But you'll look at me with a foreigner's eyes
The magical city a
Younger girl's city, a
Fantasy long since put down

EVA

All you've done to me - was that a young girl's fantasy?
I played your city games alright - didn't I?
I already know what cooks, how the dirty city feels
    and looks
I tasted it last night, didn't I?
I'm going to be a part of B.A. - Buenos Aires - Big Apple!

FAMILY

She's going to be a part of B.A. - Buenos Aires - Big Apple!

MAGALDI

Eva beware your ambition
It's hungry and cold, can't be controlled, will run wild
This in a man is a danger enough
But you are a woman, not
Even a woman, not
Very much more than a child and whatever you say
I'll not steal you away!

4. BUENOS AIRES

EVA and MAGALDI arrive in Buenos Aires

EVA

What's new Buenos Aires?
I'm new - I want to say I'm just a little stuck on you
You'll be on me too!

I get out here Buenos Aires
Stand back - you ought to know what'cha gonna get in me
Just a little touch of star quality!
Fill me up with your heat, with your noise, with your
    dirt, overdo me
Let me dance to your beat, make it loud, let it hurt,
    run it through me
Don't hold back you are certain to impress
Tell the driver this is where I'm staying

Hello Buenos Aires!
Get this - just look at me, dressed up somewhere to go
We'll put on a show!

Take me in at your flood, give me speed, give me lights,
    set me humming

Shoot me up with your blood, wine me up with your
    nights, watch me coming
All I want is a whole lot of excess
Tell the singer this is where I'm playing

Stand back Buenos Aires!
Because you ought to know what'cha gonna get in me
Just a little touch of star quality!

And if ever I go too far
It's because of the things you are
Beautiful town - I love you
And if I need a moment's rest
Give your lover the very best
Real eiderdown - and silence

CHE

On the 9th February 1935, in Buenos Aires - a polo
match, between a team of leading Argentine players and
the touring British side. The British ambassador said he
had never seen a social occasion quite like it. Even by the
standards of Buenos Aires society the gathering at the
polo ground glittered. The Rolls' and the Daimlers, the
hampers from Harrod's, the clothes, the diamonds, the
crystal, the wines, the procession of nannies from
England and France. The result of the match? Oh yes -
the home team won, but as the British ambassador
pointed out, that did not reflect badly on British
horsemanship. Three of the Argentine players were
educated at Eton.

EVA

You're a tramp, you're a treat, you will shine to the
    death, you are shoddy
But you're flesh, you are meat, you shall have every
    breath in my body
Put me down for a lifetime of success
Give me credit - I'll find ways of paying

Rio de la Plata! Florida! Corrientes! Neuve de Julio!
All I want to know!

Stand back Buenos Aires!
Because you oughta know what'cha gonna get in me
Just a little touch of
Just a little touch of
Just a little touch of star quality!

5. GOODNIGHT AND THANK YOU
CHE
(To MAGALDI)

Goodnight and thank you Magaldi
You've completed your task, what more could we ask
Of you now?
Please sign the book on your way out the door
That will be all
If we need you we'll call
But I don't think that's likely somehow

EVA

Oh but it's sad when a love affair dies
The parting, the closing of doors
But we must be honest, stop fooling ourselves

CHE

Which means - up yours!

CHE and MAGALDI

There is no-one, no-one at all
Never has been and never will be a lover
Male or female
Who hasn't an eye on
In fact they rely on

Tricks they can try on
Their partner
They're hoping their lover will help them or keep them
Support them, promote them
Don't blame them
You're the same

CHE
(To EVA's FIRST LOVER)

Goodnight and thank you whoever
She's in every magazine, been photographed, seen
She is known
We don't like to rush but your case has been packed
If we've missed anything
You could give us a ring
But we don't always answer the phone

EVA

Oh but it's sad when a love affair dies
But when we were hot we were hot
I know you'll look back on the good times we've shared

CHE

But Eva will not!

CHE, EVA, MAGALDI, EVA's FIRST LOVER

There is no-one, no-one at all
Never has been and never will be a lover
Male or female
Who hasn't an eye on
In fact they rely on
Tricks they can try on
Their partner
They're hoping their lover will help them or keep them
Support them, promote them
Don't blame them, you're the same

CHE
(To EVA's SECOND LOVER)

Goodnight and thank you whoever
We are grateful you found her a spot on the sound
Radio
We'll think of you every time she's on the air
We'd love you to stay
But you'd be in the way
So do up your trousers and go

EVA

Oh but it's sad when a love affair dies
The decline into silence and doubt
Our passion was just too intense to survive

CHE

For God's sake get out!

*By now a fairly long line of EVA's rejected LOVERS
has formed*

LOVERS

Oh but this line's an embarrassing sight
Someone has made us look fools
Argentine men call the sexual shots
Someone has altered the rules

CHE

Fame on the wireless as far as it goes
Is all very well, but every girl knows
She needs a man she can monopolize
With fingers in dozens of different pies...

LOVERS

Oh but it's sad when a love affair dies

6. THE ART OF THE POSSIBLE

Five members of the G.O.U., a right-wing grouping of officers within the military government that seized power in Argentina in 1943, including Colonel Juan PERON, are seen moving slowly back and forth in rocking chairs. During this sequence, every time the music stops, the officers rise and one chair is removed. By the end of the scene there is just one chair left, occupied by PERON.

OFFICERS

One has no rules
Is not precise
One rarely acts
The same way twice
One spurns no device
Practising the art of the possible

One always picks
The easy fight
One praises fools
One smothers light
One shifts left to right
It's part of the art of the possible

While the officers continue their game of political musical chairs, EVA appears, script in hand, at a microphone.

EVA
(on the air)

I'm only a radio star with just one weekly show
But speaking as one of the people I want you to know
We are tired of the decline of
Argentina with no sign of
A government able to give us the things we deserve

OFFICERS

One always claims
Mistakes were planned
When risk is slight

One takes one's stand
With much sleight of hand
Politics - the art of the possible

One has no rules
Is not precise
One rarely acts
The same way twice
One spurns no device
Politics - the art of the possible

VOICES

Peron! Peron! Peron!

7. CHARITY CONCERT / I'D BE SURPRISINGLY GOOD FOR YOU

Backstage at the Luna Park Stadium. EVA, by now a successful actress, and PERON, by now one of the most powerful men in the military government, are both present. EVA's old friend MAGALDI is finishing his act on stage.

MAGALDI

On this night....

CHE

Luna Park Stadium, Buenos Aires, January 22nd 1944

MAGALDI

On this night....

CHE

A concert in aid of the victims of an earthquake that devastated the town of San Juan, Argentina

MAGALDI

On this night of a thousand stars
Let me take you to heaven's door
Where the music of love's guitars
Plays for evermore!

CHE

Ladies and gentlemen! Agustin Magaldi! Any minute now - the man of the hour!

Magaldi comes off stage and runs into EVA

MAGALDI

Eva Duarte!

EVA

Your act hasn't changed much

MAGALDI

Neither has yours

Magaldi leaves. The crowd begins to call for PERON. PERON pushes his way onto the stage.

PERON

Tonight I'm proud to be the people's spokesman! You've given help to those who've lost their homes, but more than that conclusively shown that the people should run their affairs on their own! Make sure your leaders understand the people!

CROWD

Peron! Peron! Peron!

Peron leaves the stage and finds himself face to face with EVA

EVA

Colonel Peron?

PERON

Eva Duarte?

EVA and PERON

I've heard so much about you!
I'm amazed for I'm only an actress (a soldier)
Nothing to shout about (One of the thousands)
Only a girl on the boards (Defending the country he loves)

EVA

But when you act, the things you do affect us all

PERON

But when you act, you take us away from the squalor of
the real world - Are you here on your own?

EVA

Yes

PERON

So am I - what a fortunate coincidence. Maybe you're my
reward for my efforts here tonight

EVA

It seems crazy but you must believe
There's nothing calculated, nothing planned
Please forgive me if I seem naive
I would never want to force your hand
But please understand
I'd be good for you

I don't always rush in like this
Twenty seconds after saying hello
Telling strangers I'm too good to miss
If I'm wrong I hope you'll tell me so
But you really should know
I'd be good for you
I'd be surprisingly good for you
I won't go on if I'm boring you
But you do understand my point of view
Do you like what you hear, what you see, and would
    you be
Good for me too?

I'm not talking of a hurried night
A frantic tumble then a shy goodbye
Creeping home before it gets too light
That's not the reason that I caught your eye
Which has to imply
I'd be good for you
I'd be surprisingly good for you

PERON

Please go on - you enthrall me!
I can understand you perfectly
And I like what I hear, what I see, and knowing me
i would be good for you too

EVA

I'm not talking of a hurried night
A frantic tumble then a shy goodbye
Creeping home before it gets too light
That's not the reason that I caught your eye
Which has to imply
I'd be good for you
I'd be surprisingly good for you

EVA AND PERON
(But neither seems aware that the other is singing)

There is no-one, no-one at all
Never has been and never will be a lover
Male or female
Who hasn't an eye on

In fact they rely on
Tricks they can try on
Their partner
They're hoping their lover will help them or keep them
Support them, promote them
Don't blame them, you're the same

8. ANOTHER SUITCASE IN ANOTHER HALL

EVA and PERON arrive at PERON'S apartment.
PERON'S 16-year-old MISTRESS is in bed.

EVA

Hello and goodbye!
I've just unemployed you
You can go back to school - you had a good run
I'm sure he enjoyed you
Don't act sad or surprised, let's be friends, civilised
Come on little one!
Don't sit there like a dummy!
The day you knew would arrive is here - you'll survive
So move, funny face!
I like your conversation - you've a catchy turn of phrase

EVA turns PERON's MISTRESS out into the hall.

MISTRESS

I don't expect my love affairs to last for long
Never fool myself that my dreams will come true
Being used to trouble I anticipate it
But all the same I hate it - wouldn't you?
So what happens now?

CHE

Another suitcase in another hall

MISTRESS

So what happens now?

CHE

Take your picture off another wall

MISTRESS

Where am I going to?

CHE

You'll get by, you always have before

MISTRESS

Where am I going to?
Time and time again I've said that I don't care
That I'm immune to gloom, that I'm hard through
and through
But every time it matters all my words desert me
So anyone can hurt me - and they do
So what happens now?

CHE

Another suitcase in another hall

MISTRESS

So what happens now?

CHE

Take your picture off another wall

MISTRESS

Where am I going to?

CHE

You'll get by, you always have before

MISTRESS

Where am I going to?
Call in three months' time and I'll be fine I know
Well maybe not that fine, but I'll survive anyhow
I won't recall the names and places of this sad occasion
But that's no consolation - here and now
So what happens now?

CHE

Another suitcase in another hall

MISTRESS

So what happens now?

CHE

Take your picture off another wall

MISTRESS

Where am I going to?

CHE

You'll get by, you always have before

MISTRESS

Where am I going to?

CHE

Don't ask anymore

9. PERON'S LATEST FLAME

CHE

At the watering-holes of the well-to-do
I detect a resistance to

ARISTOCRATS

Precisely!

CHE

Our heroine's style

ARISTOCRATS

We're glad you noticed

CHE

The shooting sticks of the upper class

ARISTOCRATS

Give her an inch...

CHE

Aren't supporting a single arse
That would rise for the girl

ARISTOCRATS

...she'll take a mile
Such a shame she wandered into our enclosure
How unfortunate this person has forced us to be blunt
No, we wouldn't mind seeing her in Harrod's
But behind the jewellery counter - not in front

CHE

Could there be in our fighting corps
A lack of enthusiasm for

ARMY

Exactly!

CHE

Peron's latest flame?

ARMY

You said it brother

CHE

Should you wish to cause great distress
In the tidiest officer's mess
Just mention her name

ARMY

That isn't funny
Peron is a fool, breaking every taboo
Installing the girl in the army H.Q.
And she's an actress! The last straw
Her only good parts are between her thighs
She should stare at the ceiling, not reach for the skies
Or she could be his last whore
The evidence suggests
She has other interests
If it's her who's using him
He's exceptionally dim
Bitch! Dangerous Jade!

ARISTOCRATS

We have allowed ourselves to slip
We have completely lost our grip
We have declined to an all-time low
Tarts have become the set to know

ARMY

It's no crime for officers to do as they please
As long as they're discreet and keep clear of disease
We ignore, we disregard
But once they allow a bit on the side
To move to the centre where she's not qualified
We should all be on our guard
She should get into her head
She should not get out of bed
She should know that she's not paid
To be loud but to be laid
Slut! Dangerous Jade!

*EVA, the glamorous movie star, enters,
flanked by HEAVIES*

CHE
(in the guise of a reporter)

This has really been your year Miss Duarte
Tell us where you go from here Miss Duarte
Which are the roles that you yearn to play
Whom did you sleep - dine with yesterday?

EVA

Is that the extent of your interest in me?
It shows how futile acting must be

CHE

Can we assume then that you'll quit? Is this because of
your association with Colonel Peron?

HEAVIES

Goodnight and thank you
(They push CHE aside and EVA out)

ARMY

She won't be kept happy by her nights on the tiles
She says it's his body but she's after his files
So get back onto the street!
She should get into her head
She should not get out of bed
She should know that she's not paid
To be loud but to be laid
The evidence suggests
She has other interests
If it's her who's using him
He's exceptionally dim

ARISTOCRATS

Things have reached a pretty pass
When someone pretty lower class
Graceless and vulgar, uninspired
Can be accepted and admired

10. A NEW ARGENTINA

PERON

Dice are rolling, the knives are out
Would be presidents are all around
I don't say they mean harm, but they'd each give an arm
To see us six feet under ground

EVA

It doesn't matter what those morons say
Our nation's leaders are a feeble crew
There's only twenty of them anyway
What is twenty next to millions who
Are looking to you?
All you have to do is sit and wait
Keeping out of everybody's way
We'll - you'll be handed power on a plate
When the ones who matter have their say
And with chaos installed
You can reluctantly agree to be called

PERON

There again we could be foolish
Not to quit while we're ahead
For distance lends enchantment
And that is why
All exiles are distinguished
More important they're not dead
I could find job satisfaction
In Paraguay

EVA

This is crazy defeatist talk
Why commit political suicide?
There's no risk, there's no call
For any action at all
When you have unions on your side

WORKERS' VOICES

Peron! Peron!

CHE

A new Argentina!
The chains of the masses untied!
A new Argentina!
The voice of the people cannot be denied!

EVA

There is only one man who can lead any workers' regime
He lives for your problems, he shares your ideals
    and your dream
He supports you for he loves you, understands you,
    is one of you
If not - how could he love me?

MOB

A new Argentina!
The workers' battle song!
A new Argentina!
The voice of the people rings out loud and long!

EVA

Now I am a worker I've suffered the way that you do
I've been unemployed and I've starved and I hated it too
But I found my salvation in Peron - may the nation
Let him save them as he saved me

CHE

A new Argentina!
A new age about to begin!

CHE and SECRET POLICE

A new Argentina!
We face the world together and no dissent within

(The SECRET POLICE lay into CHE)

INDIVIDUAL WORKERS

Nationalisation of the industries that the foreigners
    control
Participation in the profits that we make
Shorter hours, higher wages, votes for women, larger
    dole
More public spending, a bigger slice of every cake

PERON

It's annoying that we have to fight elections for our cause
The inconvenience - having to get a majority
If normal methods of persuasion fail to win us applause
There are other ways of establishing authority

SECRET POLICE

We have ways of making you vote for us, or at least of
    making you abstain

EVA

Peron has resigned from the army and this we avow
The descamisados are those he is marching with now!
He supports you for he loves you, understands you,
    is one of you
If not - how could he love me?

ALL

A new Argentina!
The chains of the masses untied!
A new Argentina!
The voice of the people cannot be, and will not be,
    and must not be, denied!

PERON

There again we could be foolish
Not to quit while we're ahead
I can see me many miles away
Inactive
Sipping cocktails on a terrace
Taking breakfast in bed
Sleeping easy, doing crosswords
It's attractive

EVA

Don't think I don't think like you, I often get those
    nightmares too
They always take some swallowing
Sometimes it's very difficult to keep momentum if
It's you that you are following
Don't close doors
Keep an escape clause
Because we might lose
The Big Apple
But - would I have done what I did
If I hadn't thought, if I hadn't known
We would take the country?

ALL

A new Argentina!
The chains of the masses untied!
A new Argentina!
The voice of the people cannot be, and will not be,
    and must not be, denied!

(END OF ACT ONE)

ACT TWO

11. ON THE BALCONY OF THE CASA ROSADA/ DON'T CRY FOR ME ARGENTINA

PERON has just won a sweeping victory in the 1946 Presidential Election. This is the first public appearance by PERON and EVA since that triumph. Action takes place both inside and outside the balcony of the Casa Rosada (the pink Presidential Palace in Buenos Aires)

CHE

People of Argentina! Your newly elected President -
    Juan Peron!

The CROWD begins to chant "Peron! Peron!"

PERON

Argentinos! Argentinos! We are all shirtless now!
Fighting against our common enemies -
Poverty, social injustice, foreign domination of
    our industries!
Reaching for our common goals -
Our independence, our dignity, our pride!
Let the world know that our great nation is awakening
and that its heart beats in the humble bodies of Juan
Peron - and his wife, the first lady of Argentina,
Eva Duarte de Peron!

CHE

As a mere observer of this tasteless phenomenon, one has
to admire the stage management -

(heavies move in on CHE)

There again - perhaps I'm more than a mere observer
-listen to my enthusiasm, gentlemen! Peron! Peron!
-Look, if I take off my shirt, will you -

(heavies bundle CHE away)

*The CROWD by now are beginning to chant
"Evita! Evita!"*

EVA

It won't be easy, you'll think it strange
When I try to explain how I feel
That I still need your love after all that I've done
You won't believe me
All you will see is a girl you once knew
Although she's dressed up to the nines
At sixes and sevens with you

I had to let it happen, I had to change
Couldn't stay all my life down at heel
Looking out of the window, staying out of the sun
So I chose freedom
Running around trying everything new
But nothing impressed me at all
I never expected it to

Don't cry for me Argentina
The truth is I never left you
All through my wild days
My mad existence
I kept my promise
Don't keep your distance

And as for fortune, and as for fame
I never invited them in
Though it seemed to the world they were all I desired
They are illusions
They are not the solutions they promised to be
The answer was here all the time
I love you and hope you love me

Don't cry for me Argentina…

(EVA breaks down; the CROWD take up her tune)

EVA

Don't cry for me Argentina
The truth is I never left you
All through my wild days
My mad existence
I kept my promise
Don't keep your distance

Have I said too much? There's nothing more I can think
    of to say to you
But all you have to do is look at me to know that every
    word is true

*(The CROWD are ecstatically enthusiastic; EVA goes
inside from the balcony)*

Just listen to that! The voice of Argentina! We are
    adored! We are loved!

OFFICER

Statesmanship is more than entertaining peasants

EVA

We shall see, little man

CROWD

Evita Peron! La Santa Peronista!

(EVA goes back onto the balcony)

EVA

I am only a simple woman who lives to serve Peron in his
noble crusade to rescue his people! I was once as you are
now! I have taken these riches from the oligarchs only for
you - for all of you! One day you will inherit these
treasures! Descamisados! When they fire those cannons,
when the crowds sing of glory, it is not just for Peron,
but for all of us! All of us!

AN ARISTOCRAT

Things have reached a pretty pass
When someone pretty lower class
Can be accepted and admired -

EVA

But your despicable class is dead! Look who they are calling
    for now!

12. HIGH FLYING, ADORED

CHE

High flying, adored, so young, the instant queen, a
Rich beautiful thing of all the talents, a cross between a
Fantasy of the bedroom and a saint
And you were just a backstreet girl
Hustling and fighting
Scratching and biting
High flying, adored, did you believe in your wildest
    moments
All this would be yours, that you'd become the lady
    of them all?
Were there stars in your eyes when you crawled in
    at night
From the bars, from the sidewalks
From the gutter theatrical?
Don't look down, it's a long long way to fall

High flying, adored, what happens now, where do you
    go from here?
For someone on top of the world, the view's not exactly
    clear
A shame you did it all at twenty-six

There are no mysteries now
Nothing can thrill you
No-one fulfill you
High flying, adored, I hope you come to terms with
    boredom
So famous, so easily, so soon, is not the wisest thing
    to be
You won't care if they love you, it's been done before
You'll despair if they hate you
You'll be drained of all energy
All the young who've made it would agree

EVA

High flying, adored, I've been called names but they're
    the strangest
My story's quite usual, local girl makes good,
    weds famous man
I was slap in the right place at the perfect time
Filled a gap - I was lucky
But one thing I'll say for me
No-one else can fill it like I can

13. RAINBOW HIGH

EVA

I don't really think I need
The reasons why I won't succeed
I haven't started!
Let's get this show on the road
Let's make it obvious
Peron is off and rolling

EVA'S DRESSERS

Eyes! Hair! Mouth! Figure! Dress! Voice! Style!
Movement! Hands! Magic! Rings! Glamour! Face!
Diamonds! Excitement! Image!

EVA

I came from the people
They need to adore me
So Christian Dior me
From my head to my toes
I need to be dazzling
I want to be Rainbow High!
They must have excitement
And so must I

EVA'S DRESSERS

Eyes! Hair! Mouth! Figure! Dress! Voice! Style! Movement!

EVA

I'm their product
It's vital you sell me
So Machiavell-me
Make an Argentine Rose!
I need to be thrilling
I want to be Rainbow High!
They need their escape
And so do I

EVA'S DRESSERS

Eyes! Hair! Mouth! Figure! Dress! Voice! Style!
Movement! Hands! Magic! Rings! Glamour! Face!
Diamonds! Excitement! Image!

EVA

All my descamisados expect me to outshine the enemy -
    the aristocracy
I won't disappoint them!
I'm their saviour!
That's what they call me

So Lauren Bacall me
Anything goes
To make me fantastic
I have to be Rainbow High
In magical colours -

You're not decorating a girl for a night on the town!
And I'm not a second-rate queen getting kicks with
    a crown!
Next stop will be Europe!
The Rainbow's gonna tour
Dressed up, somewhere to go
We'll put on a show!
Look out, mighty Europe!
Because you oughta know what'cha gonna get in me
Just a little touch of
Just a little touch of
Argentina's brand of
Star quality!

14. RAINBOW TOUR

*PERON and some of his OFFICERS reflect on EVA's
European progress. CHE takes over many of the
OFFICERS' lines during this sequence and also adds
various comments of his own.*

PERON

People of Europe! I send you the Rainbow of Argentina!

CHE / OFFICERS

Spain has fallen to the charms of Evita
She can do what she likes - it doesn't matter much
She's the New World Madonna with the golden touch
She filled a bull-ring - forty-five thousand seater
But if you're prettier than General Franco
That's not hard

Franco's reign in Spain should see out the forties
So you've just acquired an ally who
Looks as secure in his job as you
More important, current political thought is
Your wife's a phenomenal asset
Your trump card

PERON AND OFFICERS

Let's hear it for the Rainbow Tour
It's been an incredible success
We weren't quite sure, we had a few doubts

CHE

Would Evita win through?

PERON AND OFFICERS

But the answer is yes!

EVA *(in Spain)*

There you are, I told you so
Makes no difference where we go
The whole world over - just the same
You should have heard them call our name
And who would underestimate the actress now?

PERON

I'm not underestimating you - just do the same thing in
    Italy please

CHE / OFFICERS

Now I don't like to spoil a wonderful story
But the news from Rome is not so good
She hasn't gone down like we thought she would
Italy's unconvinced by Argentine glory
They equate Peron with Mussolini
Can't think why

EVA *(in Italy)*

Did you hear that?
They called me a whore!
They actually called me a whore!

AN ITALIAN ADMIRAL (CHE)

But Signora Peron -
It's an easy mistake
I'm still called an admiral
Yet I gave up the sea long ago

CHE / OFFICERS

Things aren't all that bad she met with the Pope
She got a Papal decoration and a kindly word
So even if the crowds gave our lady the bird
The Argentine / Italy axis does have some hope
She still made a fabulous impact
Caught the eye

PERON AND OFFICERS

Let's hear it for the Rainbow Tour
It's been an incredible success
We weren't quite sure, we had a few doubts

CHE

Would Evita win through?

PERON AND OFFICERS

But the answer is -

CHE

A qualified --

PERON AND OFFICERS

Yes!

CHE / OFFICERS

Eva started well, no question, in France
Shining like the sun through the post-war haze
A beautiful reminder of more carefree days
She nearly captured the French, she sure had the chance
But she suddenly seemed to lose interest
She looked tired

PERON AND OFFICERS

Tired? Eva tired?

CHE

Face the facts, the Rainbow's started to fade
I don't think she'll make it to England now

PERON

It wasn't on the schedule anyhow

CHE

You'd better get out the flags and fix a parade
Some kind of coming home in triumph
Is required

PERON AND OFFICERS

Let's hear it for the Rainbow Tour
It's been an incredible success
We weren't quite sure, we had a few doubts
Would Evita win through?

CHE

And the answer is -

PERON AND OFFICERS

Yes

CHE

And no

PERON AND OFFICERS

And yes

CHE

And no

PERON AND OFFICERS

And yes...and no
Let's hear it for the Rainbow Tour
It's been an incredible success...

EVA *(back from Europe)*

Who the hell does the King of England think he is?
Tea at some tinpot castle of his - what kind of invitation
    is that?
Argentina's First Lady deserves Buckingham Palace!
If England can do without me
Then Argentina can do without England!

15. THE ACTRESS HASN'T LEARNED
(THE LINES YOU'D LIKE TO HEAR)

ARISTOCRACY

Thus all fairy stories end
Only an actress would pretend
Affairs of state are her latest play
Eight shows a week two matinées
My how the worm begins to turn
When will the chorus girl ever learn?
My how the worm begins to turn
When will the chorus girl ever learn?

EVA

The chorus girl hasn't learned the lines you'd like to hear
She won't go scrambling over the backs of the poor to be
    accepted
By making donations - just large enough - to the correct
    charity
She won't be president of your wonderful society of
    philanthropy
Even if you asked her to be
As you should have asked her to be

The actress hasn't learned the lines you'd like to hear
She won't join your clubs, she won't dance in your halls
She won't help the hungry once a month at your tombolas
She'll simply take control as
You disappear

CHE

Forgive my intrusion but fine as those sentiments sound
Little has changed for us peasants down here on the
    ground
I hate to seem churlish, ungrateful, I don't like to moan
But do you now represent anyone's cause but your own?

EVA

Everything done will be justified by my Foundation

16. AND THE MONEY KEPT ROLLING IN (AND OUT)

CHE *(and WORKERS on choruses)*

And the money kept rolling in from every side
Eva's pretty hands reached out and they reached wide
Now you may think it should have been a voluntary cause
But that's not the point my friends
When the money keeps rolling in you don't ask how

Think of all the people guaranteed a good time now
Eva's called the hungry to her - open up the doors!
Never been a fund like the Foundation Eva Peron!

Rolling rolling rolling
Rolling on in

Would you like to try a college education?
Own your landlord's house, take the family on vacation?
Eva and her blessed Fund can make your dreams come
    true
Here's all you have to do my friends
Write your name and your dream on a card or a pad
    or a ticket
Throw it high in the air and should our lady pick it
She will change your way of life for a week or even two
Name me anyone who cares as much as Eva Peron!

Rolling rolling rolling
Rolling on out

And the money kept rolling out in all directions
To the poor to the weak to the destitute of all
    complexions
Now cynics claim a little of the cash has gone astray
But that's not the point my friends
When the money keeps rolling out you don't keep books
You can tell you've done well by the happy grateful looks
Accountants only slow things down, figures get in
    the way
Never been a lady loved as much as Eva Peron!

Rolling rolling rolling
Rolling on out

If the money keeps rolling in what's a girl to do?
Cream a little off the top for expenses - wouldn't you?
But where on earth can people hide their little piece of
    Heaven?
Thank God for Switzerland
Where a girl and a guy with a little petty cash between
    them
Can be sure when they deposit no-one's seen them
Oh what bliss to sign your cheques as
    three-o-one-two-seven
Never been accounts in the name of Eva Peron!

Rolling rolling rolling
Rolling on in

17. SANTA EVITA

CHILDREN

Please, gentle Eva, will you bless a little child?
For I love you - tell Heaven I'm doing my best
I'm praying for you, even though you're already blessed
Please, mother Eva, will you look upon me as your own?
Make me special, be my everything wonderful perfect
    and true
And I'll try to be exactly like you
Please, holy Eva, will you feed a hungry child?
For I love you - tell Heaven I'm doing my best....

CHE

Get them while they're young, Evita, get them while they're
    young!

CHILDREN

....I'm praying for you, even though you're already blessed

WORKERS

Santa Santa Evita
Madre de todos los ninos
De los tiranizados

De los descamisados
De los trabajadores
De la Argentina

CHE

Why try to govern a country when you can become a saint?

18. WALTZ FOR EVA AND CHE

CHE

Tell me before I waltz out of your life
Before turning my back on the past
Forgive my impertinent behaviour
But how long do you think this pantomime can last?
Tell me before you ride off in the sunset
There's one thing I never got clear
How can you claim you're our saviour
When those who oppose you
Are stepped on, or cut up, or simply disappear?

EVA

Tell me before you get onto your bus
Before joining the forgotten brigade
How can one person like me, say,
Alter the time-honoured way the game is played?
Tell me before you get onto your high horse
Just what you expect me to do
I don't care what the bourgeoisie say
I'm not in business for them but to give all my
    descamisados
A magical moment or two

CHE AND EVA

There is evil, ever around, fundamental
System of government quite incidental

EVA

So what are my chances
Of honest advances?
I'd say low
Better to win
By admitting my sin
Than to lose with a halo

CHE

Tell me before I seek worthier pastures
And thereby restore self-esteem
How can you be so short-sighted
To look never further than this week or next week
To have no impossible dream?

EVA

Allow me to help you slink off to the sidelines
I'll pay for your fare, give three cheers
But first tell me who'd be delighted
To witness me tackle
The world's greatest problems
From war to pollution?
No hope of solution
Even if I lived for one hundred years

CHE AND EVA

There is evil, ever around, fundamental
System of government quite incidental

EVA

So go, if you're able
To somewhere unstable
And stay there
Whip up your hate
In some tottering state
But not here, dear

Is that clear, dear?

Oh what I'd give for a hundred years!
But the physical interferes
Every day more - O my Creator!
What is the good of the strongest heart
In a body that's falling apart?
A serious flaw - I hope You know that

19. SHE IS A DIAMOND

OFFICERS

It's all very well - to a certain extent
For the lady at the side of the President
To show an interest in affairs
But let's not be blind to the drift of events
She's eclipsing the strength of the government
She should return to below stairs
She will never win our hearts
She's a woman for a start
She holds no elected post
She's an ornament at most

CHE

What's new Buenos Aires? Your nation, which a few years
ago had the second largest gold reserves in the world, is
bankrupt! A country which grew up and grew rich on
beef is rationing it! La Prensa, one of the few newspapers
which dares to oppose Peronism, has been silenced, and
so have all other reasonable voices! I'll tell you what's
new Buenos Aires!

PERON (to OFFICERS: CHE has gone)

But on the other hand - she's all they have
She's a diamond in their dull grey lives - and that's the
Hardest kind of stone - it usually survives
And if you think about it, can you recall
The last time they loved anyone at all?

She's not a bauble you can brush aside
She's been out doing what we just talked about - example
Gave us back our businesses, got the English out
And when you think about it - well why not do
One or two of the things we promised to?

But on the other hand she's slowing down
She's lost a little of that magic drive - but I would
Not advise her critics present to derive
Any satisfaction from her fading star
She's the one who's kept us where we are

OFFICERS

She's the one who's kept you where you are

20. DICE ARE ROLLING

PERON

Dice are rolling, the knives are out
I see every bad sign in the book
And as far as they can - overweight to a man!
They have that lean and hungry look

EVA

But we still have the magic we've always had! The
descamisados still worship me - we arrived thanks to
them and no-one else; no thanks to your generals - a
clutch of stuffed cuckoos!

PERON

It's not a question of a big parade, proving we're big with
the mobs on the street -

EVA

You're wrong - the people, my people -

PERON

The people belong to no-one! They are fickle, can be manipulated, they don't matter! However much they love you now it matters more that as far as my stuffed cuckoos are concerned, you don't politically exist!

EVA

So I don't exist! So I count for nothing! Try saying that on the street when all over the world I am Argentina!
(EVA breaks off for a second - in some pain)

Most of your generals wouldn't be recognized by their own mothers! But they'll admit I exist when I become vice-president!

PERON

That won't work...we've been through all of this before, they'd fight you tooth and nail - you'd never overcome them with a hundred rallies and even if you did -

EVA

Yes?

PERON

Your little body's slowly breaking down
You're losing speed, you're losing strength - not style -
     that goes on
Flourishing forever, but your eyes, your smile
Do not have the sparkle of their fantastic past
If you climb one more mountain it could be your last

EVA

I'm not that ill - bad moments come but they go
Some days are fine, some a little bit harder
But that does not mean
I should change my routine
Have you ever seen
Me defeated?
Don't you forget what I've been through and yet
I'm still standing
And if I am ill - that could even be to your advantage!

PERON

Advantage? I'm trying to point out that you are dying!

This talk of death is chilling - of course you're not going
     to die!

EVA

Then I must now be vice-president!

And I shall have my people come to choose
Two Perons to wear their country's crowns
In thousands in my squares and avenues
Emptying their villages and towns
Where every soul in home or shack or stall
Knows me as Argentina - that is all

O I shall be a great vice-president!

(But EVA collapses in great pain)

PERON

So what happens now?

So what happens now?

EVA

Where am I going to?

PERON

Don't ask any more

21. EVA'S FINAL BROADCAST

CHE

Forgive my intrusion, Evita, I just have to see
How you admit you have lost - a brand new experience-
     - we
Got it set up! We fixed you a broadcast - and you're so
     good on the air!

EVA

The actress hasn't learned the lines you'd like to hear
How could she feel defeated by such cringing
     mediocrities?
She's sad for her country
Sad to be defeated by her own weak body
She's sad for her people
She hopes they will know she did not betray them

(A microphone is switched on - she is now on the air)

I want to tell the people of Argentina
I've decided I should decline
All the honours and titles you've pressed me to take
For I'm contented - let me simply go on
As the woman who brings her people to the heart of
     Peron!
Don't cry for me Argentina
The truth is I shall not leave you
Though it may get harder
For you to see me
I'm Argentina
And always will be

Have I said too much? There's nothing more I can think
     of to say to you
But all you have to do is look at me to know that every
     word is true

22. MONTAGE

*(In her last hours, images, people and events from EVA's
life flow through her mind, while the grief of the nation
knows no bounds)*

CHE

She had her moments - she had some style
The best show in town was the crowd
Outside the Casa Rosada crying, "Eva Peron"
But that's all gone now...

MAGALDI

Eva beware your ambition...

EVA

Screw the middle classes! I will never accept them and they will never deny me anything again. My father's other family were middle class, and we were kept out of sight, hidden from view....

It seems crazy but you must believe
There's nothing calculated, nothing planned
Please forgive me if I seem naive
I would never want to force your hand
But please understand...

CROWD

A new Argentina!
The chains of the masses untied!
A new Argentina!
The voice of the people cannot be and will not be
     and must not be...

PERON

High flying, adored, so young, the instant queen, a
Rich beautiful thing of all the talents, a cross between a
Fantasy of the bedroom and a saint...

CROWD

Santa Santa Evita
Madre de todos los ninos...

CHE

Sing you fools but you've got it wrong
Enjoy your prayers because you haven't got long
Your queen is dead, your king is through
She's not coming back to you!

CROWD

...de los tiranizados
De los descamisados
De los trabajadores
De la Argentina

23. LAMENT

EVA

The choice was mine and mine completely
I could have any prize that I desired
I could burn with the splendour of the brightest fire
Or else - or else I could choose time
Remember I was very young then
And a year was forever and a day
So what use could fifty, sixty, seventy be?
I saw the lights and I was on my way

And how I lived! How they shone!
But how soon the lights were gone!

Oh my daughter! Oh my son!
Understand what I have done!

(The moment EVA dies EMBALMERS move in to preserve her fragile body)

EMBALMERS

Eyes, hair, face, image
All must be preserved
Still life displayed forever
No less than she deserved

CHE

Money was raised to build a tomb, a monument to Evita. Only the pedestal was completed and Evita's body disappeared for seventeen years.

THE END

Andrew Lloyd Webber and Tim Rice began working on EVITA in 1974, their first collaboration for the musical theater since JESUS CHRIST SUPERSTAR.

In 1976, the first recording of the work was released as a double album on MCA Records, produced by the authors and featuring Julie Covington as Eva Peron, Colm Wilkinson as Che and Paul Jones as Juan Peron. The album was a number one record in many countries of the world as was a single of *"DON'T CRY FOR ME ARGENTINA"* performed by Julie Covington. Only in North America was this original recording less than successful, where its release remained a closely-guarded secret until fairly recently. No less than four other songs from the musical, *"ANOTHER SUITCASE IN ANOTHER HALL", "OH WHAT A CIRCUS", "I'D BE SURPRISINGLY GOOD FOR YOU"* and *"ON THIS NIGHT OF A THOUSAND STARS"* have subsequently hit various best-seller charts around the world.

On June 21, 1978 the first staging of EVITA took place, at the Prince Edward Theatre in London. The Robert Stigwood-David Land production was directed by Harold Prince, choreographed by Larry Fuller, designed by Tim O'Brien and Tazeena Firth, and starred Elaine Paige as Eva Peron, David Essex as Che and Joss Ackland as Juan Peron. The London Cast album of EVITA repeated the success of the 1976 studio recording by earning a gold record within weeks of its release in Britain. EVITA the show has won numerous awards including the important Society of West End Theatre Award as Best Musical of 1978, Elaine Paige winning the S.W.E.T. Award for Best Performance in a Musical. At the time of the writing of this note (September 1979) EVITA in London has played to standing room only ever since its opening night.

On May 8, 1979 the American premiere of EVITA took place at the Dorothy Chandler Pavilion, Los Angeles, as part of the Los Angeles Civic Light Opera's 42nd Annual Season. This production starred Patti LuPone as Eva Peron, Mandy Patinkin as Che and Bob Gunton as Juan Peron, and after 9 weeks in Los Angeles and a further seven at the Orpheum Theatre in San Francisco, moved to Broadway, Robert Stigwood and David Land, Harold Prince, Larry Fuller, Tim O'Brien and Tazeena Firth (among others) repeating their London tasks. This Premiere American Recording of the entire work was released in the U.S. and Canada in September 1979 and features the performers of the American stage production. Those familiar with the original 1976 recording will note that Andrew Lloyd Webber and Tim Rice have made several alterations (they hope improvements) to EVITA since then.

Available on MCA Records and Tapes